Poemas de Las Madres
The Mothers' Poems

Eastern Washington University Press

Gabriela Mistral
Poemas de Las Madres
The Mothers' Poems

❖

Translation by Christiane Jacox Kyle

❖

Paintings by Sara Adlerstein González

❖

Introduction by Margaret Sayers Peden

EWU
P·R·E·S·S
EASTERN
WASHINGTON
UNIVERSITY

Cheney, Washington, 1996

LIBRARY OF CONGRESS CATALOGING-IN-PUBLICATION DATA

MISTRAL, GABRIELA, 1899-1957.
    POEMAS DE LAS MADRES = THE MOTHERS' POEMS / TRANSLATION BY
CHRISTIANE JACOX KYLE ; PAINTINGS BY SARA ADLERSTEIN GONZÁLEZ ;
INTRODUCTION BY MARGARET SAYERS PEDEN.
        P.   CM.
    ISBN 0-910055-29-7
    1. MOTHERS--POETRY.   I. JACOX KYLE, CHRISTIANE, 1950-
II. ADLERSTEIN GONZÁLEZ, SARA, 1952-   .   III. TITLE.
PQ8097.G6P55   1996
861--DC20   96-3605
                                                            CIP

Printed in Korea through Amica International

For Our Mothers

and

For Our Children

and for

Doris Dana, with Gratitude

POEMAS DE LAS MADRES

INTRODUCTION

Gabriela Mistral is Latin America's best-known and most beloved woman poet since the time of Sor Juana Inés de la Cruz, the famous seventeenth-century Mexican nun. Like Sor Juana, Mistral was fortunate enough to be appreciated in her lifetime. Like Sor Juana, Mistral rose from extremely humble origins to enjoy international acclaim, and both earned their renown within rigidly male-dominated cultures. Each was precocious as a child and largely self-taught, and each greatly advanced the stature of women in her time.

There comparisons should end, for Gabriela Mistral, born in 1889, [d. 1957] is the product of vastly different times and circumstances from those of a seventeenth century vice-royalty. Had Mistral been born a century later, in the age of television, she surely would have inspired a mini-series, for the life of this woman, who is the first Latin American, male or female, to have been awarded the Nobel Prize for Literature, is the stuff of which dramas are made. She was born Lucila Godoy y Alcayaga, in a small provincial town in Chile. (She chose her pseudonym from the name of the archangel Gabriel and that of the mistral, the violent wind that blows through the Rhone Valley of France.) Mistral's biography has been colored by anecdote and legend, so that it is difficult to be precise about her early years, but we know they would not ordinarily lead to the distinction she achieved. She rarely mentioned her nearly illiterate mother, and her father, of whom she wrote fondly, has been referred to both as "a distinguished teacher" and as a "schoolmaster," unemployed at the time of her birth and given to periodic "absences" in search of adventures. The most dramatic legend of Mistral's life is that of a tragic death she wrote about in *Sonetos de la Muerte [Sonnets of Death]*. For years the story circulated that she had written these poems in her grief over the suicide of her lover, Romelio Ureta. Later in her life, however, while not denying that influence, Mistral insisted that Ureta had not killed himself over her, that their relationship had come to an end before his death, that by then he was engaged to a girl chosen for him by his older brother, and that actually he had killed himself out of shame for a financial indiscretion, not for love of *any* woman.

Legends about Gabriela Mistral pale, however, beside her reality. An autodidact—she entered school when she was five, and was teaching by the time she was fifteen—Mistral was in 1922 invited by Mexico's revolutionary Secretary of Education, Jose Vasconcelos, to come to Mexico to assist him in organizing that nation's entire system of rural education. Her own teaching career had advanced—despite any formal training—by having the normal requirements waived. A woman who considered the Christian Bible the greatest of all books, and who wrote of it, "How many times have you comforted me/ As many times as I have been laid low," spent twenty years of her life as a Buddhist. A woman from a country whose male hierarchy dominated every phase of life, Mistral served as Chile's ambassador in Madrid, Lisbon, Nice, Brazil, Mexico City and New York, and also as its representative at the United Nations. A woman known as a great poet of Chile and the Spanish language, her first collection of poems, *Desolación, 1922,* was published in the United States under the auspices of a distinguished professor at Columbia University, Federico de Onis. But perhaps the greatest irony in Mistral's life was this childless woman's lifelong dedication to children, a passion—nearly obsession—readily visible in her poems, as well as in her long career as an elementary educator. Fernando Alegria has called Mistral a "peripatetic educational mission," who left a trail of schools behind her.

Gabriela Mistral cut a striking figure. Her photographs show a tall, large-boned, ramrod-straight woman with strong features: coal-black, arched eyebrows over equally black, sad but expressive eyes; a prominent Roman nose; black-turning-to-white hair cut short and combed back from her face in gentle waves; a mouth usually captured in a mood of willful self-control. Mistral always dressed very plainly, in dark suits and sensible shoes, without jewelry or ornamentation of any kind. Not beautiful, she was a handsome and impressive woman, and those who knew her uniformly commented on her presence.

The prose poems in *Poemas De Las Madres/The Mothers' Poems* illustrate perfectly Mistral's sense of sisterhood with all women—none more binding than with women fortunate enough to have borne children. We read her almost uncanny sense of empathy in "What Will He Be Like?" sense the gravid weight of her unborn child in "Sensitive"— "I'm like a branch heavy with fruit" —share her mother-to-be's fears in "Tell Me, Mother." These moments are made even more bittersweet when we hear behind them and through them Mistral's grief over the teenage suicide of the nephew she had adopted as a child.

If ever a writer's deepest emotions and wishes were revealed in her writing, we see them here. Poet, educator, diplomat, Nobel Laureate, role model, humanitarian, Lucila Godoy y Alcayaga offers us her flesh, her creation, in these *Mothers' Poems*. And we know that everyone, male or female, birth mother or loving human, can share with her the empathic joy and pain of motherhood.

—Margaret Sayers Peden

Margaret Sayers Peden, Professor Emerita of Spanish, University of Missouri, Columbia, has been accorded many distinctions and awards as teacher, translator, and scholar. She is the translator of Carlos Fuentes, Isabel Allende, Pablo Neruda, Octavio Paz, and many others. *Woman of Genius,* her translation of the critical autobiography of Sor Juana Inès de la Cruz, is included in *The Norton Anthology of World Masterpieces,* and will shortly be published with her translations of *Primero Sueño* and *Selected Poems* by Sor Juana (Viking Penguin, 1996).

TRANSLATOR'S NOTE

When I first read Gabriela Mistral's *The Mothers' Poems*, I was deeply moved by the voice of the young woman, and intrigued by the cadences of her speech, by Mistral's immense gift with the human voice. I wanted to understand how Mistral was able to combine such sweet clarity with such complexity of emotion and context. I wanted to carry the generous spirit of that voice into English.

In translating these prose poems, two writers served as guides for me. Muriel Rukeyser called translation "Treason and resurrection and bringing over. It is a mythological effort to bring a music over into another life . . . It is a working through the flesh. With all its mistakes, it's like bringing up a child." To bring the music over meant finding the sounds and patterns of speech, the physical level by which meaning is conveyed in poetry, that would embody the young woman's voice in English. At the same time, I held to Mario Susko's belief that translation is "an act of love, a presentation and a remaking of the language of one culture for that of another, not to erase differences but to leave the traces, so that otherness may be embraced." The act of translation is one of balancing, like love, separation and connection, the same themes the young woman explores throughout *The Mothers' Poems*.

The greatest challenge was to honor the complexities of Mistral's language, which is one of the sources of her great power as a writer, because it allows her to express the complexities of the human heart in relationship to the world. She knew this about her work— "I came out of a labyrinth of hills and something of this knot that cannot be untied remains in whatever I do, whether poetry or prose." Her imagery can be multilayered as she adds qualifier upon qualifier, like Russian dolls enveloping one another. Because Spanish is more flexible than English in the placement of phrases and clauses, I added words in the English to keep the relationship of the images clear, as in "As if I were a cluster of blue grapes, the light passed slowly through me, to deliver its sweetness." ("Wisdom"). But I admit I was most moved by the intricacies of Mistral's music. She captures the absolute song of the heart with all its catches and halts and flights, and she accomplishes this through her choice of specific words and phrases, syntactical order and even punctuation. I wanted first to carry over the vowel music, at times substituting a different sound, as in "For I am weaving in this silence, in this quiet, a body, a miraculous body, with veins and face, and gaze, and purest heart" ("Quiet"), where I chose the lengthening sound of the long "a" in English for the growing fullness of the long "o" in Spanish. I tried to hold to the Biblical cadences which lean the work into the mythological level. I attempted this by maintaining the syntactical and phrasal order whenever I could without wrenching the English. Those units of meaning and of breath are in relationship to each other, and to the other units around them, much as a line in poetry is in tension with other lines, and with its syntax. To keep Mistral's order sometimes meant keeping a sense of otherness, a slight wrenching, as in "One who loved, and whose love asked, when she received the kiss, for eternity" ("Sacred Law"). A more natural English phrasing would have been "asked for eternity," but the separation signifies the time the whole prose sequence encompasses—the pregnancy—between the asking and the receiving of eternity in the child's birth. And finally, I chose to use Mistral's punctuation as much as possible, which compels us to read line breaks so that the poetry of the young woman's life can barely be contained in the prose.

There were two texts available, the sequence as it first appeared in *Desolación*, Mistral's first collection, which was published in 1922 by the Instituto de las Españas, and the revised version published in 1950 by Editorial de Pacifico as a separate limited edition with illustrations by André Racz. Mistral claimed herself to be revising constantly, and it was a delight to see the meticulous care she seems to have taken. The changes are consistent. She eliminated unnecessary adjectives, as in "and if his straight hair has the simplicity of my [whole] life" ("What Will he Be Like?"). She altered punctuation, or connective language, not so much to alter meaning, but to catch the right rhythmic pattern to underscore meaning, in keeping with my sense that she used punctuation to create line breaks. And, finally, she moved what was originally an endnote, an extended comment on the significance of the sequence for herself and for the world, from the end of the poems to the beginning. In this way Mistral carried her own commitment and intentions for the text forward, placing the young woman's story into the world, as a mother carries a child forth and introduces that child to the world. This subtle act of claiming resonates through the text, making the young woman's story less isolated and more significant because of Mistral's profound intentions.

The latter edition had originally caught my eye because of the illustrations, and when I met with Doris Dana to discuss the translations, she suggested bringing the poems forward in time with a contemporary Latin American artist's work. I hoped to find a Chilean woman, believing the works might speak more intimately to one another across time. Finding Sara Adlerstein González was a small miracle; not only was her work exceptional, but in our first conversation she said she knew *The Mothers' Poems*, and believed she had completed paintings which would speak with the poems. On an afternoon in Seattle, between the Cascades—our own version of the Cordillera—and the Pacific, the same geography Mistral lived between and loved, Sara, Jim McAuley and I placed the paintings beside the prose poems, created at least ten thousand miles and seventy-five years apart, as if they'd been done in complete concert.

Together, these works are a testament to those who recognize our global responsibility towards the children we all share, our sacred trust which Gabriela Mistral understood so well when she wrote "May they feel the deep tenderness of this woman who, as she wanders the earth nurturing the children of others, sees the mothers of all the children of the world."

—Christiane Jacox Kyle

TABLE OF CONTENTS

Poemas de Las Madres

—Una tarde, paseando por una calle miserable de Temuco, vi a una mujer del pueblo, sentada a la puerta de su *rancho*. Estaba próxima a la maternidad, y su rostro revelaba una profunda amargura.

Pasó delante de ella un hombre, y le dijo una frase brutal, que la hizo enrojecer.

Yo sentí en ese momento toda la solidaridad del sexo, la infinita piedad de la mujer para la mujer, y me alejé pensando:

—Es una de nosotras quien debe decir (ya que los hombres no lo han dicho) la santidad de este estado doloroso y divino. Si la misión del arte es embellecerlo todo, en una inmensa misericordia, ¿por qué no hemos purificado, a los ojos de los impuros, *esto?*

Y escribí los poemas, con intención casi religiosa.

Algunas de esas mujeres que para ser castas necesitan cerrar los ojos sobre la realidad cruel pero fatal, hicieron de estos poemas un comentario ruin, que me entristeció, por ellas mismas. Hasta me insinuaron que los eliminase de un libro.

En esta obra egotista, empequeñecida a mis propios ojos por ese egotismo, tales prosas humanas tal vez sean lo único en que se canta la Vida total. ¿Había de eliminarlas?

¡No! Aquí quedan, dedicadas a las mujeres capaces de ver que la santidad de la vida comienza en la maternidad, la cual es, por lo tanto, sagrada. Sientan ellas la honda ternura con que una mujer que apacienta por la Tierra los hijos ajenos, mira a las madres de todos los niños del mundo!

The Mothers' Poems

—One afternoon, walking along a miserable street in Temuco, I saw a village woman sitting in the doorway of her shack. She was very pregnant, and her face revealed a profound bitterness.

A man walked by her, and made a crude remark, and she blushed.

At that moment I felt all the solidarity of sex, the infinite pity of woman for woman, and I went away thinking:

—One of us ought to speak (since men haven't done so) of the sacredness of this painful and divine condition. If the purpose of art is to make everything beautiful, with an immense mercy, why haven't we purified, for the eyes of the impure, *this?*

And I wrote these poems with an almost religious intention.

Some of those women who, in order to be pure, have to shut their eyes to the pain of real life, made vicious comments about the poems, which saddened me, for their sake. They even insinuated I shouldn't publish them.

In this selfish work, diminished in my own eyes by this selfishness, perhaps such human stories might be the only place where all Life sings. Should they not exist?

No! Here they are, dedicated to women capable of seeing that the sacredness of life begins in motherhood, which is, in itself, sacred. May they feel the deep tenderness of this woman who, as she wanders the earth nurturing the children of others, sees the mothers of all children of the world!

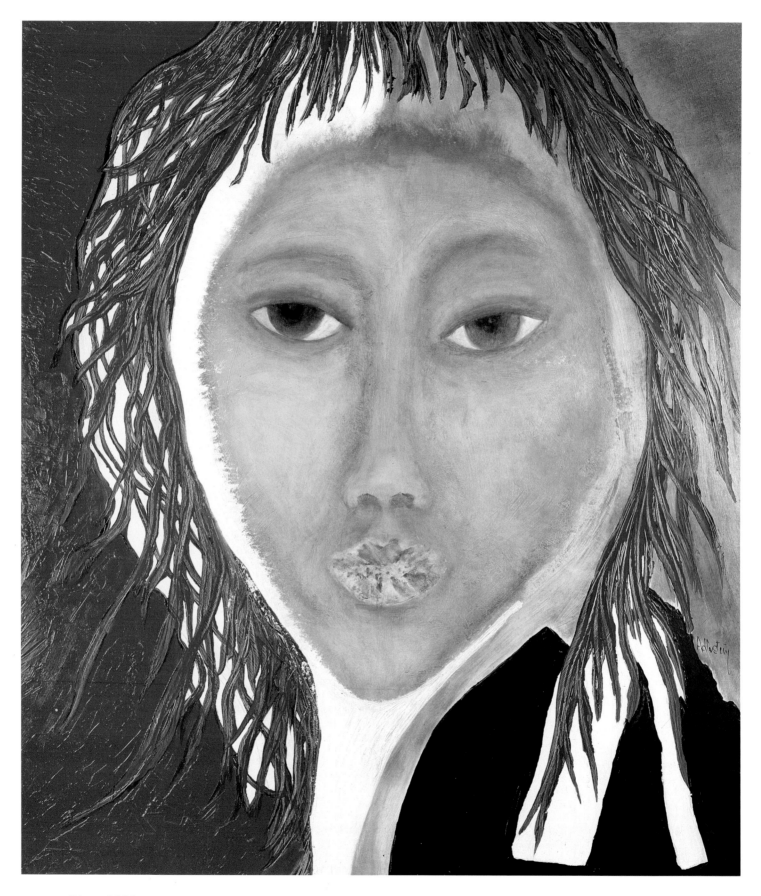

Diosa del Monte

Me Ha Besado

Me ha besado y ya soy otra: otra, por
el latido que duplica el de mis venas y
por el aliento que se percibe entre mi
aliento. Mi vientre ya es noble como mi
corazón...

Y hasta encuentro en mi hálito una
exhalación de flores: ¡todo por aquél que
descansa en mis entrañas blandamente,
como el rocío sobre la hierba!

He Kissed Me

He kissed me, and now I'm another;
another because of the pulse that dupli-
cates the pulse of my veins and because
of the breath perceived within my
breath. Now my womb is noble, like
my heart...

And I even discover the smell of
flowers on my breath: all this because
of that one who rests softly in my center
like dew on the grass!

Visualities

¿CÓMO SERÁ?

¿Cómo será? Yo he mirado largamente los pétalos de una rosa, los palpé con delectación: querría esa suavidad para sus mejillas. Y he jugado en un enredo de zarzas, porque me gustarían sus cabellos así, oscuros y retorcidos. Pero no importa si es tostado, con ese rico color de las gredas rojas que aman los alfareros, y si sus cabellos lisos tienen la simplicidad de mi vida.

Miro las quiebras de las sierras, cuando se van poblando de niebla, y hago con la niebla una silueta de niña, de niña dulcísima: que pudiera ser eso también.

Pero, por sobre todo, yo quiero que mire con el dulzor que él tiene en la mirada, y que tenga el temblor de su voz cuando me habla, pues en el que viene quiero amar a aquél que me besara.

WHAT WILL HE BE LIKE?

What will he be like? I've studied the petals of a rose for hours. I touched them with delight: I would want that softness for his cheeks. And I've played in a tangle of blackberries because I would want his hair like that, dark and curly. But it won't matter if it's brown, that rich color of the fuller's red clay that the potters love, and if his straight hair has the simplicity of my life.

I study the cragged mountains when they fill with mist, and I form the silhouette of a girl, the sweetest girl, with the mist: so the child could be that also.

But, more than anything, I want his child to have the sweetness of his gaze, and have the tremor of his voice when he speaks with me, because in the one who comes I want to love the one who kissed me.

La Que soy, La Que no soy

SABIDURÍA

Ahora sé para qué he recibido veinte veranos la luz sobre mí y me ha sido dado cortar las flores por los campos. ¿Por qué, me decía en los días más bellos, este don maravilloso del sol cálido y de la hierba fresca?

Como el racimo azulado, me traspasó la luz para la dulzura que entregaría. Este que en el fondo de mí está haciéndose gota a gota de mis venas, éste era mi vino.

Para éste yo recé, por traspasar del nombre de Dios mi barro, con el que se haría. Y cuando leí un verso con pulsos trémulos, para él me quemó como una brasa la belleza, por que recoja de mi carne su ardor inextinguible.

WISDOM

Now I know why I've received the light of twenty summers on me, and why I've been given to picking flowers along the fields. Why, I asked myself on the most beautiful days, this marvelous gift of the warm sun and fresh grass?

As if I were a cluster of blue grapes, the light passed slowly through me, to deliver its sweetness. This which is making itself deep within me, drop by drop from my own veins, this was my wine.

For this one I prayed, so the name of God would pass through my clay, from which he would be made. And when I read a verse with trembling hands, He made my beauty burn like a red hot coal, so He could gather, for this child, his inextinguishable ardor from my flesh.

La Vida En Rosa

LA DULZURA

Por el niño dormido que llevo, mi paso se ha vuelto sigiloso. Y es religioso todo mi corazón, desde que lleva el misterio.

Mi voz es suave, como una sordina de amor, y es que temo despertarlo.

Con mis ojos busco ahora en los rostros el dolor de las entrañas, para que los demás miren y comprendan la causa de mi mejilla empalidecida.

Hurgo con miedo de ternura en las hierbas donde anidan codornices. Y voy por el campo silenciosa, cautelosamente: creo que árboles y cosas tienen hijos dormidos, sobre los que velan inclinados.

SWEETNESS

Because of the sleeping child I carry, my step has become secretive. And my whole heart is holy since it began carrying this mystery.

My voice is soft, like a mute love song, and it's because I'm afraid of awakening him.

Now my eyes search faces for the sorrow deep inside, so that the others may look and understand the reason for my pale cheeks.

With fear born of tenderness, I search through the grasses where the quail make their nests. And I go through the field silently, cautiously: I believe trees and all things have sleeping children whom they hover over, keeping watch.

La Hermana

Hoy he visto una mujer abriendo un surco. Sus caderas están henchidas, como las mías, por el amor, y hacía su faena curvada sobre el suelo.

He acariciado su cintura; la he traído conmigo. Beberá la leche espesa de mi mismo vaso y gozará de la sombra de mis corredores, que va grávida de gravidez de amor. Y si mi seno no es generoso, mi hijo allegará al suyo, rico, sus labios.

My Sister

Today I've watched a woman digging a furrow. Her hips are filled out like mine, because of love, and she was bending over the ground as she worked.

I've caressed her waist; I've carried her with me. She'll drink rich milk from my own glass and rejoice in the shadow of my corridors, which is growing heavy with the weight of love. And if my breast isn't generous, my child's lips will come to the richness of hers.

El Ruego

¡Pero no! ¿Cómo Dios dejaría enjuta
la yema de mi seno, si El mismo amplió
mi cintura? Siento crecer mi pecho,
subir como el agua en un ancho
estanque, calladamente. Y su
esponjadura echa sombra como de
promesa sobre mi vientre.

¿Quién sería más pobre que yo en el
valle si mi seno no se humedeciera?

Como los vasos que las mujeres
ponen para recoger el rocío de la noche,
pongo yo mi pecho ante Dios; le doy un
nombre nuevo, le llamo el Henchidor, y
le pido el licor de la vida. Mi hijo
llegará buscándolo con sed.

My Prayer

But no! How could God leave the
bud of my breast so gaunt, if He himself
fattened my waist? I feel my breasts
swell, rise like water in a wide reservoir,
quietly, secretly. And their swollenness
casts a shadow like a promise over my
womb.

Who in the whole valley would be
poorer than me if my breast didn't fill?

Like the women who place jars
outside to gather the evening dew, I
place my breasts before God; I give
Him a new name. I call Him The One
Who Fills, and I ask Him for the liqueur
of life. My child will arrive thirsty,
looking for this.

Tristeza en do-menor

SENSITIVA

Ya no juego en las praderas y temo
columpiarme con las mozas. Soy como
la rama con fruto.

Estoy débil, tan débil que el olor de
las rosas me hizo desvanecer esta siesta,
cuando bajé al jardín. Y un simple canto
que viene en el viento o la gota de
sangre que tiene la tarde en su último
latido sobre el cielo, me turban, me
anegan de dolor. De la sola mirada de
mi dueño, si fuera dura para mí esta
noche, podría morir.

SENSITIVE

I don't play in the meadows anymore
and I'm afraid of swinging with the
young girls. I'm like a branch heavy
with fruit.

I feel weak, so weak that when I went
down to the garden this afternoon, the
smell of roses made me dizzy. And a
simple song that comes on the wind, or
the drop of blood the afternoon holds in
its final throb across the sky, troubles
me, floods me with sorrow. Just one
glance from my man, if he were harsh to
me tonight, and I could die.

Marina Salina

El Dolor Eterno

Palidezco si él sufre dentro de mí;
dolorida voy de su presión recóndita, y
podría morir a un solo movimiento de
éste a quien no veo.

Pero no creáis que únicamente estará
trenzado con mis entrañas mientras lo
guarde. Cuando vaya libre por los
caminos, aunque esté lejos, el viento que
lo azote me rasgará las carnes y su grito
pasará también por mi garganta. ¡Mi
llanto y mi sonrisa comenzarán en tu
rostro, hijo mío!

Eternal Pain

I grow pale if he suffers inside me.
I'm becoming full of pain from his
hidden pressure, and I could die from a
single movement of this one I don't see.

But don't think he'll only be woven
with my soul while I keep watch over
him. When he wanders freely out in the
streets, even though far away, the wind
that lashes at him will tear my flesh and
his cry will also rise in my throat. My
tears and my smile will begin in your
face, my child!

Tirana La Inalcanzable

Por Él

Por él, por el que está adormecido,
como hilo de agua bajo la hierba, no me
dañéis, no me déis trabajos.
Perdonádmelo todo: mi descontento de
la mesa preparada y mi odio al ruido.

Me diréis los dolores de la casa, la
pobreza y los afanes, cuando lo haya
puesto en unos pañales.

En la frente, en el pecho, donde me
toquéis está él y lanzaría un gemido
respondiendo a la herida.

Because of Him

Because of him, because of this one
who is lulled like a thread of water
under the grass, don't hurt me, don't
trouble me. Forgive me everything: my
discomfort at the table filled with food
and my hatred of noise.

Tell me about the troubles of the
household, our poverty and hard work,
when I've put him in diapers.

Wherever you touch me, on my
forehead, on my breast, he's there, and
he would wail in response to the
wound.

La Quietud

Ya no puedo ir por los caminos:
tengo el rubor de mi ancha cintura y de
la ojera profunda de mis ojos. Pero
traedme aquí, poned aquí a mi lado las
macetas con flores, y tocad la cítara
largamente: quiero para él anegarme de
hermosura.

Digo sobre el que duerme estrofas
eternas. Recojo en el corredor hora tras
hora el sol acre. Quiero destilar como la
fruta miel hacia mis entrañas. Recibo en
el rostro viento de los pinares.

La luz y los vientos coloreen y laven
mi sangre. Para lavarla también ya no
odio, no murmuro, ¡solamente amo!

Que estoy tejiendo en este silencio, en
esta quietud, un cuerpo, un milagroso
cuerpo, con venas y rostro, y mirada, y
depurado corazón.

Quiet

I can't go along the roads anymore:
I'm embarrassed by my wide waist and
the deep circles under my eyes. But
bring me here, put the clay pots filled
with flowers here beside me, and play
the zither long and slowly: I want to
flood myself with beauty for him.

I recite eternal stanzas over the one
who sleeps. Hour after hour I gather the
acrid sun on the porch. I want to distill
honey, as fruit does, into my depths. I
welcome the wind from the pine groves
in my face.

Let the light and the winds redden
and wash my blood. In order to cleanse
it, now I don't hate, I don't gossip, I only
love!

For I'm weaving in this silence, in
this quiet, a body, a miraculous body,
with veins and face, and gaze, and
purest heart.

Ropitas Blancas

Tejo los escarpines minúsculos, corto el pañal suave: todo quiero hacerlo por mis manos. Vendrá de mis entrañas, reconocerá mi perfume.

Suave vellón de la oveja: en este verano te cortaron para él. Lo esponjó la oveja ocho meses y lo emblanqueció la luna de Enero. No tiene agujillas de cardo ni espinas de zarza. Así de suave ha sido el vellón de mis carnes, donde ha dormido.

¡Ropitas blancas! Él las mira por mis ojos y se sonríe, adivinándolas suavísimas . . .

Small White Clothes

I knit tiny booties, I cut the soft diapers; I want to make everything by hand. They'll come from my depths, they'll remember my perfume.

Soft fleece of the ewe: this summer they sheared you for him. For eight months your soft wool swelled like a sponge, bleached by January's moon. It doesn't have any small thistle needles or blackberry thorns. The soft wool of my own flesh, where he has slept, is just like this.

Small white clothes! He looks at them through my eyes and smiles, imagining them to be the softest . . .

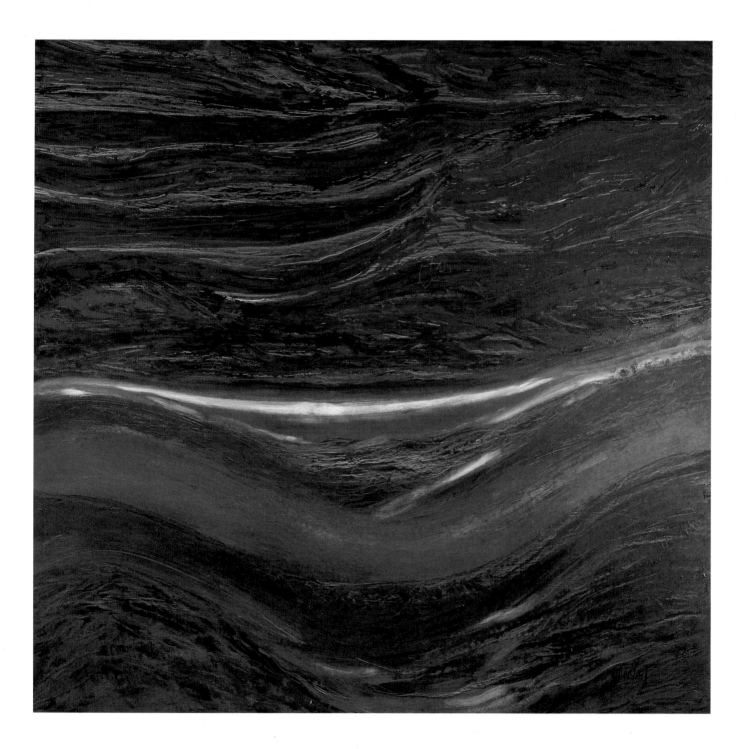

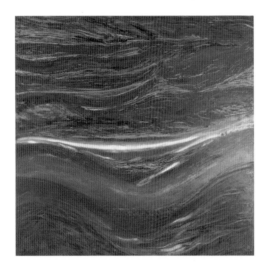 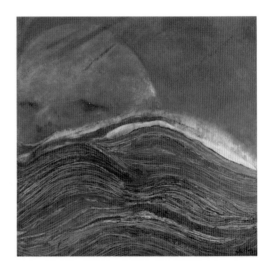

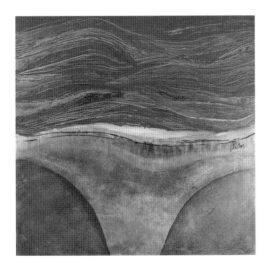

Por Cielo, Mar, y Tierra

IMAGEN DE LA TIERRA

No había visto antes la verdadera imagen de la Tierra. La Tierra tiene la actitud de una mujer con un hijo en los brazos (con sus criaturas en los anchos brazos).

Voy conociendo el sentido maternal de las cosas. La montaña que me mira, también es madre, y por las tardes la neblina juega como un niño por sus hombros y sus rodillas.

Recuerdo ahora una quebrada del valle. Por su lecho profundo iba cantando una corriente que las breñas hacen todavía invisible. Ya soy como la quebrada; siento cantar en mi hondura este pequeño arroyo y le he dado mi carne por breña hasta que suba hacia la luz.

EARTH'S IMAGE

I hadn't seen the true image of the Earth before. The Earth has the shape of a woman with a child in her arms (with her young in her wide arms).

I'm beginning to recognize the maternal feeling of things. The mountain that watches me is also mother, and in the afternoon the fog plays like a child on her shoulders and knees.

Now I remember a gorge in the valley. A stream went singing through its deep bed, completely hidden by the craggy ground covered with brambles. Now I'm like the gorge; I feel this small arroyo sing in my depths and I have given him my flesh for a cover of brambles until he comes up to the light.

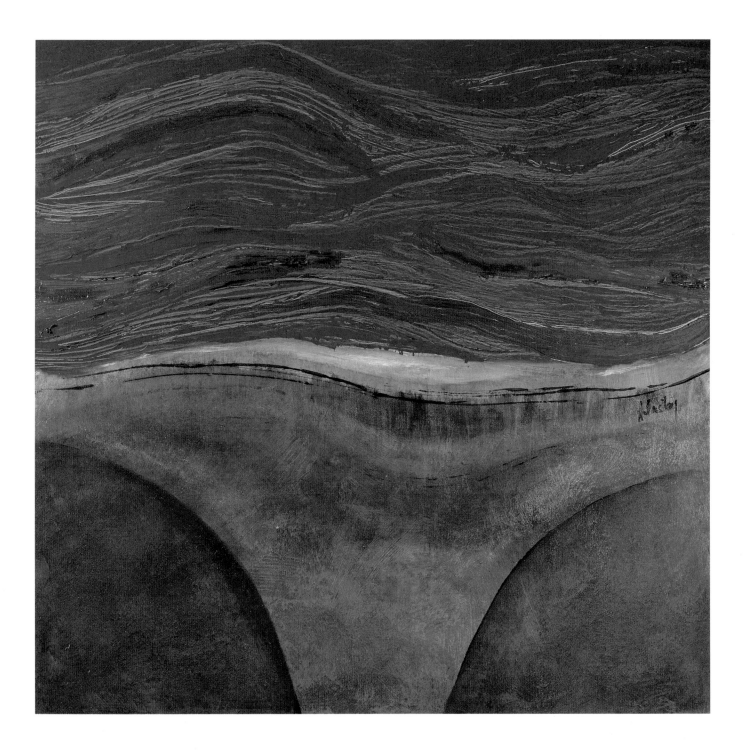

Por Cielo, Mar, y Tierra

AL ESPOSO

Esposo, no me estreches. Lo hiciste
subir del fondo de mi ser como el lirio
de aguas. Déjame ser como un agua en
reposo.

¡Ámame, ámame ahora un poco más!
Yo ¡tan pequeña! te duplicaré por los
caminos. Yo ¡tan pobre! te daré otros
ojos, otros labios, con los cuales gozarás
el mundo; yo ¡tan tierna! me hendiré
como un ánfora por el amor, para que
este vino de la vida se vierta.

¡Perdóname! Estoy torpe al andar,
torpe al servir tu copa; pero tú me
henchistes así y me diste esta extrañeza
con que me muevo entre las cosas.

Séme más que nunca dulce. No
remuevas ansiosamente mi sangre; no
agites mi aliento.

¡Ahora soy sólo un velo; todo mi
cuerpo es un velo bajo el cual duerme
un niño!

TO MY HUSBAND

Husband, don't embrace me. You
made this one rise up from the depths of
me like a water lily. Let me be like still
water.

Love me, love me now a little more!
I, so small! I'll duplicate you on all the
roads. I, so poor! I'll give you other
eyes, other lips with which you can
delight in the world; I, so tender! For
love I'll split myself open like an am-
phora so this wine of life spills out.

Forgive me! I'm clumsy when I walk,
clumsy when I serve your cup; but you
filled me like this and you gave me this
wonder with which I move among the
things of this world.

Be more gentle with me than ever.
Don't shake my blood anxiously; don't
disturb my breath.

Now I'm simply a veil; all my body
is a veil under which a child is sleeping.

La Dama Blanca

LA MADRE

Vino mi madre a verme; estuvo sentada aquí a mi lado, y, por primera vez en nuestra vida, fuimos dos hermanas que hablaron del tremendo trance.

Palpó con temblor mi vientre y descubrió delicadamente mi pecho. Y al contacto de sus manos me pareció que se entreabrían con suavidad de hojas mis entrañas y que a mi seno subía la honda láctea.

Enrojecida, llena de confusión, le hablé de mis dolores y del miedo de mi carne; caí sobre su pecho; ¡y volví a ser de nuevo una niña pequeña que sollozó en sus brazos del terror de la vida!

MY MOTHER

My mother came to see me; she was sitting beside me, and, for the first time in our lives, we were two sisters who spoke of the tremendous event.

Trembling, she touched my belly and delicately uncovered my breasts. And when her hands touched me, it seemed I opened softly as leaves somewhere deep inside, and my milk welled up from the depths to my breast.

Blushing, full of confusion, I told her of my pain and the fear in my flesh; I fell against her breasts; and I became once again the small child sobbing in her arms at the terror of life!

The Pain or the Rain?

Cuéntame, Madre . . .

Madre, cuéntame todo lo que sabes
por tus viejos dolores. Cuéntame cómo
nace y cómo viene su cuerpecillo,
entrabado con mis vísceras.

Dime si buscará solo mi pecho o si se
lo debo ofrecer, incitándolo.

Dame tu ciencia de amor ahora,
madre. Enséñame las nuevas caricias,
delicadas, más delicadas que las del
esposo.

¿Cómo limpiaré su cabecita, en los
días sucesivos? ¿Y cómo lo liaré para no
dañarlo?

Enséñame, madre, la canción de cuna
con que me meciste. Esa lo hará dormir
mejor que otras canciones.

Tell Me, Mother

Mother, tell me everything you know
from your old sorrows. Tell me how he
is born and how his tiny body comes to
be, bound with the core of my body.

Tell me if he'll search for my breast
by himself, or if I should offer it, encour-
aging him.

Give me your knowledge of love
now, mother. Teach me the new ca-
resses, delicate, more delicate than those
of a spouse.

How will I wash his little head in the
days to come? And how will I wrap him
up so I won't harm him?

Teach me, mother, that lullaby you
rocked me with. That one will make
him sleep better than any other songs.

El Amanecer

Toda la noche he padecido, toda la noche se ha estremecido mi carne por entregar su don. Hay el sudor de la muerte sobre mis sienes; pero no es la muerte, ¡es la vida!

Y te llamo ahora Dulzura Infinita a Ti, Señor, para que lo desprendas blandamente.

¡Nazca ya, y mi grito de dolor suba en el amanecer, trenzado con el canto de los pájaros!

Dawn

All night I've suffered, all night my flesh has shuddered to deliver its gift. There's the death sweat on my temples; but this isn't death, it's life!

And now I call You Infinite Sweetness, Lord, so that You might free him easily.

Be born now, and let my cry of pain rise at dawn, woven with the singing of the birds!

LA SAGRADA LEY

Dicen que la vida ha menguado en
mi cuerpo, que mis venas se vertieron
como los lagares: ¡yo sólo siento el
alivio del pecho después de un gran
suspiro!

—¿Quién soy yo, me digo, para tener
un hijo en mis rodillas?

Y yo misma me respondo:

—Una que amó, y cuyo amor pidió,
al recibir el beso, la eternidad.

Me mire la Tierra con este hijo en los
brazos, y me bendiga, pues ya estoy
fecunda como las palmas.

SACRED LAW

They say that life has waned in my
body, that my veins emptied themselves
like wine presses; I feel only the relief in
my breast after a great sigh!

—Who am I, I ask myself, to have a
child on my knees?

And I answer myself:

—One who loved, and whose love
asked, when she received the kiss, for
eternity.

Let the Earth look at me with this
child in my arms, and bless me; for, yes,
now I'm as fruitful as the palm trees.

Niña Montaña

POEMAS DE LA MADRE
MÁS TRISTE

ARROJADA

Mi padre dijo que me echaría, gritó a mi madre que me arrojaría esta misma noche.

La noche es tibia; a la claridad de las estrellas, yo podría caminar hasta la aldea próxima; pero ¿y si nace en estas horas? Mis sollozos le han llamado tal vez; tal vez quiera salir por ver mi cara. Y tiritaría bajo el aire crudo, aunque yo lo cubriera.

POEMS OF THE
SADDEST MOTHER

CAST OUT

My father said he would throw me out; he shouted at my mother that he would cast me out this very night.

The night is warm; by the clear light of the stars, I could walk to the next village; but what if he's born during these hours? Maybe my sobs have called him; maybe he would want to come out to see my face. And he would shiver in the raw wind, even though I would cover him.

Madre Tierra

¿Para Qué Viniste?

¿Para qué viniste? Nadie te amará aunque eres hermoso, hijo mío. Aunque sonríes graciosamente, como los demás niños, como el menor de mis hermanitos, no te besaré sino yo, hijo mío. Y aunque tus manitas se agiten buscando juguetes, no tendrás para tus juegos sino mi seno y la hebra de mis lágrimas, hijo mío.

¿Para qué viniste, si el que te trajo te odió al sentirte en mi vientre?

¡Pero no! Para mí viniste; para mí que estaba sola, hasta cuando me oprimía él entre sus brazos, hijo mío!

WHY DID YOU COME?

Why did you come? No one will love you, even though you're beautiful, my child. Even though you smile happily, like the other children, like the youngest of my little brothers, no one will kiss you but me, my child. And even though your small hands might search restlessly for toys, you won't have anything to play with except my breast and the thread of my tears, my child.

Why did you come, if the one who brought you to be hated you when he felt you in my womb?

But no! You came for me; for me who was alone, even when he pressed me in his arms, my child!

Acknowledgments

Eight of the translations from *Poemas de las Madres* have appeared (in slightly different versions) in the *Iowa Review,* Vol. XXIII, No. 3, 1993.

I would like to thank John Gill of Crossing Press, Perry Higman, and Doris Dana for their suggestions, encouragement, and friendship; and the Abigail Quigley McCarthy Foundation for a grant which made it possible to devote time to translating the work of Gabriela Mistral.

Without the vision and commitment—both practical and æsthetic—of Jim McAuley, this book would not have "come up into the light." He has my deepest gratitude.

—Christiane Jacox Kyle

THE TRANSLATOR

Christiane Jacox Kyle graduated *Magna Cum Laude* from Mount Holyoke College and received the M.F.A. degree in poetry from Eastern Washington University in 1981. Her verse collection, *Bears Dancing In The Northern Air*, received the 1990 Yale Younger Poets Award, and was published by Yale University Press in 1991. Her poetry has appeared in anthologies and journals throughout North America. Her many honors include a Richard Eberhart Prize, the Abigail Quigley McCarthy Associates Award, a Phi Beta Kappa prize, and several Northwest Regional Foundation grants.

Her teaching career spans twenty-five years, beginning at St. Labre Indian School in Montana. She has taught Poetry Workshops, Literature, Women's Studies, and English as a Second Language at Gonzaga University, Eastern Washington University, Yale University, and Hofstra University. She has also held positions as Director of Communications for St. Labre Education Association and Program Manager of the EWU Women's Studies Center.

Her translations from the works of Spanish and Latin-American poets have appeared in *Anthology of Magazine Verse,* Monitor, 1981, and *Love Poems from Spain and Spanish America,* City Lights, 1986, and in *International Poetry Review, Jeopardy, Willow Springs, The Iowa Review, Seneca Review,* and *Prairie Schooner. The One Tongue Of Intuition: Selected Poetry and Prose Of Gabriela Mistral,* is forthcoming from University of Texas Press.

She lives in Connecticut with her husband Charles and two daughters, Katherine and Mattie.

THE ARTIST

Sara Adlerstein González is a native of Lota, Chile. She studied biology at the University of Concepción and pursued postgraduate studies in marine biology at the University of Washington. She began her career as an artist in the early 'eighties, and was quickly recognized for her lively colors and strongly textured paintings. She is now considered by critics and among the general public in Chile as one of that country's leading artists.

Her works are included in the collections of the Museo de Arte Contemporáneo, Santiago, Pinacoteca de la Universidad de Concepción, Seattle Art Museum, Eastern Washington University, and in many private collections in the United States, Latin America, and Europe. She has been represented in many group exhibits and shown individually at galleries and museums in the United States, Chile, and France since she began showing her paintings in 1989. Among these are the Seattle Bumbershoot Festival; the Cunningham Gallery, Seattle; Sala Escuela Moderna, Santiago; Instituto Chileno-Norteamericano de Cultura, Concepción; and Le Salon des Indépendants, Grand Palais, Paris. Most recently, she exhibited her paintings at La Galerie de l'Université de Pierre et Marie Curie in Paris, with the French artist Pierre Chotin.

She lives near Hamburg, Germany, with her husband Edgar and the younger of her two sons, Jorge. Her older son, Benjamin, is attending the University of Washington. She is on the staff of Zentrum für Meers und Fischereiwissenschaft of Universität Hamburg.

Hoy en estas obras de reminiscencia figurativa junto a otras composiciones—
algunas que recuerdan paisajes—, encontramos una magia llena de encanto y
optimismo. El color logra crear mundos de intimidad brillante, a la vez sensible,
proyectándonos hacia los horizontes escondidos de nuestra imaginación.

Dr. Antonio Fernández Vilches
Director de la Pinacoteca
Universidad de Concepción.